FⱯLL HIGHER

BOOKS BY DEAN YOUNG

Fall Higher
The Art of Recklessness
The Foggist
Primitive Mentor
embryoyo
True False
Original Monkey
elegy on toy piano
Ready-Made Bouquet (U.K.)
Skid
First Course in Turbulence
Strike Anywhere
Beloved Infidel
Design with X

DEAN YOUNG
FALL HIGHER

COPPER CANYON PRESS

PORT TOWNSEND, WASHINGTON

Copper Canyon Press is in residence at Fort Worden State Park in Port Townsend, Washington, under the auspices of Centrum. Centrum is a gathering place for artists and creative thinkers from around the world, students of all ages and backgrounds, and audiences seeking extraordinary cultural enrichment.

Some of these poems have appeared previously in *The American Poetry Review*, *Crazyhorse*, *Forklift Ohio*, *jubilat*, *Narrative*, *The New Yorker*, *Poetry*, and *The Threepenny Review*. Thank you to those editors.

"Demon Cycle" can also be found interspersed with the work of six other poets who were part of the inspiration for writing it in *7 Poets, 4 Days, 1 Book*, published by Trinity University Press.

LIBRARY OF CONGRESS CATALOGING-IN-PUBLICATION DATA
Young, Dean, 1955–
Fall higher / Dean Young.
    p. cm.
ISBN 978-1-55659-311-6 (pbk. : alk. paper)
I. Title.
PS3575.O782F35 2011
811'.54—dc22
                                        2010040154
98765432 first printing

COPPER CANYON PRESS
Post Office Box 271
Port Townsend, Washington 98368
www.coppercanyonpress.org

for Laurie

hark, dumbass,

the error is not to fall
but to fall from no height

CONTENTS

1

2

3

FⱯLL HIGHER

1

Lucifer

You can read almost anything
about angels, how they bite off
the heads first, copulate with tigers,
tortured Miles Davis until he stuck
a mute in his trumpet to torture them back.
The pornographic magazines ported
into the redwoods. The sweetened breath
of the starving. The prize livestock
rolls over on her larval young,
the wooden dwarf turning in the cogs
of the clockworks. I would have
a black bra hanging from the shower rod.
I would have you up against
the refrigerator with its magnets
for insurance agents and oyster bars.
Miracles, ripped thumbnails,
everything a piece of something else,
archangelic, shadow-clawed,
the frolicking despair of repeating
decimals because it never comes out even.
Mostly the world is lava's rhythm,
the impurities of darkness
sometimes called stars. Mostly
the world is assignations, divorces
conducted between rooftops. Forever
and forever the checkbook unbalanced,
the beautiful bodies bent back
like paper clips, the discharged
blandishing cardboard signs by the exits.
Coppers and silvers and radiant traces,
gold flecks from our last brush,
brushfires. Always they're espousing
accuracy when it's accident, the arrow

not in the aimed-for heart but throat
that has the say. There are no transitions,
only falls.

Red Glove Thrown in Rosebush

If only bodies weren't so beautiful.
Even rabbits are made of firecrackers
so tiny they tickle your hand.
If only the infirmities,
blocked neural pathways, leg braces
and bandages didn't make all these bodies
look like they're dancing.
Breathing will destroy us, hearts
like ninja stars stuck into the sternums
of granite caesars. Should I worry
people have stopped saying how skinny
and pale I am? Paul may destroy the kitchen
but he's the best cook I know.
Seared tuna, pesto risotto—where
did he get those tomatoes?—what a war
must be fought for simplicity!
Even the alligator, flipped over,
is soft as an eyelid. Hans, the trapezist,
got everyone high on New Year's Eve
with a single joint, the girl he was with
a sequin it was impossible not to want
to try to catch without a net.
Across the bay, fireworks punched
luminous bruises in the fog.
If only my body wasn't borrowed from dust!

This Evening from Far Away

The jackals have their sideways reproaches,
the great-aunts their brooches crusted
with emeralds or rubies or paste, the wine

has its slowness, the commuter her haste
but inside each thing is also something other,
strange, counter, shadow of an airplane

inside the raincoat, chessman in the otter,
pirouette in the luncheonette, note
emerging two octaves out of range.

Everlasting is comrade to this moment's
flash; glance away, it's another day,
you've lost one chance but here's another,

some cash, a sublet by the water; all
this bother moving place to place, shifting
syntax, anxiety attacks, the fights

and late-night make-ups, disgrace,
mercy in the friend's face may make rich
recollection lying on the deathbed or

seconds after a head-bonk ends it
and from eternity's cracked-open lid
that first pet the vet injected

while you held a paw and wept
bounds forth as if from your own chest
to greet you.

Scarecrow on Fire

We all think about suddenly disappearing.
The train tracks lead there, into the woods.
Even in the financial district: wooden doors
in alleyways. First I want to put something small
into your hand, a button or river stone or
key I don't know to what. I don't
have that house anymore across from the graveyard
and its black angel. What counts as a proper
goodbye? My last winter in Iowa there was always
a ladybug or two in the kitchen for cheer
even when it was ten below. We all feel
suspended over a drop into nothingness.
Once you get close enough, you see what
one is stitching is a human heart. Another
is vomiting wings. Hell, even now I love life.
Whenever you put your feet on the floor
in the morning, whatever the nightmare,
it's a miracle or fantastic illusion:
the solidity of the boards, the steadiness
coming into the legs. Where did we get
the idea when we were kids to rub dirt
into the wound or was that just in Pennsylvania?
Maybe poems *are* made of breath, the way water,
cajoled to boil, says, This is my soul, freed.

Madrigal

Maybe we put too much faith in the heart
when any blockhead knows everything falls apart,
turn to mush the storied administrations of the brain,
there's no statue that won't eventually dissolve in rain,
the continents are in pieces, the empire a mess,
the fleece full of holes, the rivers distressed.
Not what we promised and swore, didn't and did,
not the terrible things that happened to us as kids
makes much diff. We're the types
who bring parasols to gunfights.
A dove backfires, a dump truck coos,
everything's out of whack since I lost you.
Worse than a job chicken-processing,
worse than a courtroom of the deaf addressing,
like trying on a shirt with the pins still in it,
listen to the heart you'll soon regret it.
The photos in their oval frames bestow blame and frown,
whatever you used all your might to heave into the air is due to
        come crashing down.
Not the hatchet job you wanted but the one you took,
you stagger from the feast for a look
at a polluted brook, rather polluted yourself.
You feel like something fallen from its shelf,
a yo-yo with a busted string, chipped ceramic elf
because all you can think about is not there,
the eyes not there, not there's hair.
You still don't know what to say
and keep saying it, still trying to give your hiding place away
making a silly commotion with the leaves
of the tree you're falling from. But once that paper's creased,
there's no uncreasing. Once the numbers are deleted,
there's nothing to add up. So time for the tarry slumber
of so what who cares what's it matter,

what should be open closes, should be soft hardens
while the next set of fools scampers into the puzzle garden
detonating with laughter.

Rock Garden

No one knows where cruelty comes from,
not if there was one to split between two
or someone fell in love with the wrong person
or god or idea or when the thornbush

pushed forth its first rose. One day the river
finds a rock in itself and it leadeth
to twisting in furious froth and the doctor
finds a rock in himself which leadeth

to twisting that sometimes helps healing,
sometimes the head just sucked further under.
But in the beginning or just before,
there was probably already enough wind

to twist everything. You don't have to drink
another shot of tequila to feel it.
Just try to get through airport security.
Check out the inexplicable foams on the beach.

It's hard to sit all day with the yellow highlighter
and US vs. whomever and its precedences
and not know you're making a losing argument.
They are millionaires in the house on the hill

but they let the baby cry and cry.
I met them once and was handed a glass
designed so if you have the slightest tremor,
you spill. There are hard things inside

each of us like gravel in a chicken's crop
or magnets that leadeth us to screaming
at shadows, yanked from one derangement
into another, slapping the face that would be pure,

but without them we probably couldn't stand up
let alone walk by those sprawled on the sidewalk
with their medical conditions advertised
on cardboard or the kids from the rich suburbs

begging for money for dope. How beautiful
their tattoos, one girl all over tigers!

Dragonfly

Whatever you start out as
you end up as something else,
the process lurches, jumps, stalls
but maybe there's balance in the ravage,
the invisible origins of music.
The left hand is thousands of years older
than the right, that's why most people
still don't know how to use it
although you'd think the opposite true
if you didn't know people lasted a second.
So what? Sugar on one side, acid on the other.
Just as the couple moves out of the house
they've lived in for years, the pear trees
he planted bloom for the first time
but someone else moves in.
And suppose they cut down those trees
for a crappy prefab gazebo. So what?
A wobbly starving dog trots along the freeway.
A girl stretches a hatchling back into the nest
but drops it. The boys in crisp white short-sleeves
and drab ties try to convert the runaway
Hare Krishnas who try to chant them into being,
the friendliest people in the world and utterly mad.
How's that puzzle coming?
Sure has a lot of sky.
Remember when the college donated
the marching band's old uniforms to the shelter?
For a while the schizo spare-changers
and filthy sleepers on steam grates
in vermilion waistcoats with two rows
of golden buttons, epaulets and tails.
I don't think suffering is necessary
for beauty like my mother did

but she won the argument. Lorca, I'd plead.
Lorca, she'd rest her case. Debussy? Debussy.
So that's the bargain? With bricks
someone somehow builds a waterfall.
The guy who hoses the slaughterhouse floor
goes home and makes angels out of toothpicks.
I've lost so much tackle in this stream
you'd think I'd give up.

Selected Recent and New Errors

My books are full of mistakes
but not the ones Tony's always pointing out
as if correct spelling is what could stop the conveyor belt
the new kid caught his arm in.
Three weeks on the job and he's already six hundred
legal pages, lawyers haggling in an office
with an ignored view of the river
pretending to be asleep, pretending
to have insight into its muddy self.
You think that's a fucked-up, drawn-out metaphor,
try this: if you feel like you're writhing like a worm
in a bottle of tequila, you don't know
it's the quickness of its death that reveals
the quality of the product, its proof.
I don't know what I'm talking about either.
Do you think the dictionary ever says to itself
I've got these words that mean completely
different things inside myself
and it's tearing me apart?
My errors are even bigger than that.
You start taking down the walls of your house,
sooner or later it'll collapse
but not before you can walk around
with your eyes closed, rolled backwards
and staring straight into the amygdala's meat locker
and your own damn self hanging there.
Do that for a while and it's easier to delight
in snow that lasts about twenty minutes
longer than a life held together
by the twisted silver baling wire
of deception and stealth.
But I ain't confessing nothing.
On mornings when I hope you forget my name,

I walk through the high wet weeds
that don't have names either.
I do not remember the word *dew*.
I do not remember what I told you
with your ear in my teeth.
Farther and farther into the weeds.
We have absolutely no proof
god isn't an insect
rubbing her hind legs together to sing.
Or boring into us like a yellow jacket
into a fallen, overripe pear.
Or an assassin bug squatting over us,
shoving a proboscis right through
our breastplate then sipping.
How wonderful our poisons don't kill her.

Opal

It's not that Monet cared that much about stacks of hay.

Your feelings will never change, you'll just stop paying so much
　　　attention.

A whole summer's songs go by, the whole house turns blue.

A friend will need some help carrying boxes to the curb.

So slowly you'll reach into the pond's reflection of your own face—
　　　as if reaching into your face!—the tiny fishes will brush your
　　　fingers like nerves made of water.

Someone else will have to be young enough to climb the scaffolding
　　　around the town hall to derange all four of its clock faces.

The same laughter will have to work the rest of your life.

A friend takes your arm in the woods, it's darker turning back.

You point at an opal in a glass case and the person behind it is only
　　　too glad to let you see it against your skin but it's someone
　　　else's skin you want.

You didn't get everything but you got a lot.

Fucked-Up Ode

We all know that moment when the woman
lays her hand on the man's scar. We have all
heard water pouring in Brahms, wrens twitter
in the flowering bush. Still we don't
understand each other? What a lot
of practice it takes making the howling
face blank. We manage the couch up the stairs'
right angle, we've touched each other
exactly right, both touching and being touched
but then we miss each other by seconds
which is all chaos needs. It's not just mis-
hearing that makes us shout what we don't mean,
throw money on the table and leave. Always
too much and not enough, all those workbooks
full of calculations worthless. We swore
each day we'd check the tadpoles, threw
the knife so far into the air, we forgot
to keep watch for it coming back down.
How many letters are being crumpled up
right now? I find myself saying I love you
to almost nothing, to fog. Can't we
go back to being children with keys
looped on string around our necks?

The Usual Decision-Making Process

All day I gather signs: my scars shine,
a rope ladder hangs from a bolted window,
in the corner store a shimmering robe
drapes a headless, hollow monster
and I still think of your body.
On my table a ladybug searches
for someplace to cram herself
like a note she didn't want to know
she'd written. It only gets dark
half the sky at a time. An hour later,
my watch, glowing, hasn't moved.
Earlier, I think, the river showed me
places to disappear but it was fooling itself,
the river wasn't going anywhere. Impossible
to cut out your own heart but if you do,
maybe you'll grow another.

Irrevocable Ode

When you finally admit you're broken,
Can I come back up now? asks the chair
with its leg snapped in the basement
and Don't even get me started, says the sky.
After a while what always spun can't
without a raw rasp. Exhausted with tears
and rage, the couple look at each other,
shrug, half a face almost smiling.
Smiling the mechanic coming toward us,
wiping his greasy hands on a greasier rag,
shaking his head. Not no exactly, no
inexactly and one year the waxwings
don't appear where they always have.
You knock and knock at a door, it won't
open anymore, the paint blisters and peels
and that too you'll learn is beautiful.
When Rikyū gave his richest patron
a crude clay teapot, it had already
been broken twice. The knee never heals
and when it rains…. The wife can't forget
what the husband drunkenly raved,
the diamond cutter his miscalculations,
the contractor thinks if only a few hundred
more rivets, just a couple more thou….
If only I hadn't trusted or trusted
sooner, if I hadn't tried to pass on the hill.
Broken vow, broken silence with a coyote's howl.
And you who didn't get your cat to the vet
in time, who dozed, who messed up
your sister's wedding yelling at your mom,
who made a friend cry as a joke, jammed
the disposal with the antique, pearl-handled
spoon, who let someone else take the blame,

spiller of red wine on white rugs,
breaker of others' bones, parachuter,
big talker, lover of fire, dumb creature
of ice, maybe you won't be forgiven,
maybe you'll never find all your pieces,
a new home, maybe you'll search and petition
and wander until you're heard from no more.

Sleeping Aid

Do you wake up sooner than you go to sleep?
Do you have trouble falling?
Is your heart made of fire but your mouth ash?
Do you think of your life as a black hole
and everything hurried along,
every amphibian, every eyelash
hurried along?
What other drugs are you taking?
Can you spit them out?
A tiny cathedral lodged in your lung?
The sequence of heads wrapped in barbed wire
that is your genealogy?
Whose trachea is that lying in the road?
Whose English teacher is that lying in the road?
What blank is yours to fill in
regarding the worm's intestines?
How can you withstand the termites' gnawing,
popsicle stick, the true cross, makes no diff,
gnawing?
Are you avoiding the sun?
Hang up a minute.
Would you like something sweet?
I don't think it's counterindicated.
You may feel weak.
Perceive an errant sheen.
A stinging in the palms.
If you're planning on staying alive,
a glass of water brought down the hall
by a known hand is a boon.
It's not the skricket of the cricket
but its silence that is clairvoyant.
Someone's shaking out a great plastic sack
until it nearly pops with empty satisfaction.

Because it's just a children's book,
maybe the terrible things happening
are only there for the funny drawings.
Well, it's colder than we thought
standing by the window. And the basement?
The cat's found someplace warm to vanish.

Commencement Address

I love you for shattering.
Someone has to. Just as someone
has to announce inadvertently
the end of grief or spring's
splurge even as the bureaucrat's
spittoon overflows. Someone has to come out
the other end of the labyrinth
saying, What's the big deal?
Someone has to spend all day staring
at the data from outer space
or separating the receipts
or changing the sheets in sour room after room.
I like it when the end of the toilet paper
is folded into a point.
I like napkins folded into swans
because I like wiping my mouth on swans.
Matriculates, come back from the dance floor
to sip at the lachrymal glands of chaos,
a god could be forgiven
for eating you, you've been such angels
just not very good ones.
You've put your tongue
into the peanut canister
of your best friend's girlfriend's mom.
You've taken a brown bag lunch
on which was writ a name not your own.
All night it snows a blue snow
like the crystallized confessions
you've wrung from phantoms
even though it's you wearing the filched necklace,
your rages splitting the concrete like dandelions.
All that destruction from a ball of fluff!
There's nothing left but hope.

Fate

We may have had a choice just not known it.
The churchgoer says, Oh heck, the agnostic, God damn it.
Spring expresses reluctance
but we feel released on our own recognizance,
of what we'll be tried and probably convicted
we'll stay in the dark like lesser angels evicted.
Afoul of laws known and unknown seems fundament
but so are kisses following breath mints.
I try to say I love you but it's already said,
let's forget we never met.
Of it all, fall into bed or compost pit,
rising like smoke, dying fire given a poke,
it's up to us to make of the most,
to hack out a garden, plant a fence post,
hurl ourselves into each new task and pleasure
with varying parts abandon and measure,
playlist of Bach, Thrasher, and Thelonious Monk,
giddy drunks and peevish, plummeting funks,
hotel wake-ups, in-the-alley shots,
heart-thrumming signature, accidental blots,
wanting never to lose what we miraculously found
then smashing it down down down,
a shirt that can't be washed because it has your smell,
burning your letters, telling you to go to hell,
to hold what can't be held,
to be strongest, fastest, firstest but to yield,
cried-apart eve, laugh-patched morn,
the memory of your beautiful snore.
Every arrival delayed, departing
rerouted, strangers to ourselves and everyone else sparking
from the awful I-can't-go-on tension,
luminous with yes-sexy friction.

Omen Ode

Can't you feel it coming like the rumble
of a delivery truck blocks off or an earth-
quake, not after- but before-shock, cat's
ears cocked, snakes leaving their holes?

First glimpse of the girl on the snowy bridge,
his life is over and so too just begins,
an echo that comes first as now he thinks
it's always been. Out of nowhere achoo,

premonitions of the flu. How *do* you
recognize your favorite song backwards
on the radio contest? Is guessing future's
déjà vu, aleatory fact not aftermath or

abstract, exact as a lark's call or book
falling open to the verb of today's
conjugations in a mess of tenses
as off you go on your blind date with fate,

what makes you late and miss your bus
fortuitously. Maybe there are no accidents
but there sure are crashes, heart-stop that starts
the businessman over as a painter, the other

he always would have been now is, memory
flashing not backwards, i.e. not over
but forward. Maybe a million strings connect
tomorrow to now, not puppetry

but better yet neural net sending blips,
jolts, inklings of tiny bells, itching
in the ears, funny sting in the fingertips,
what I knew I'd know but know I didn't,

not late but later, before ever-after.
PS prelude: I've been expecting you.

Vintage

Because I will die soon, I fall asleep
during the lecture on the ongoing
emergency. Because they will die soon,
the young couple has another baby.
She's not out yet but it's late enough
to see her struggle like a dancer
in a big bubble. Because the puppy
will die soon, he learns not to pee
on the carpet. The nuisance of forget-me
flowers weed-whipped in the roaring late
summer, the mold perfect on the grapes
for zinfandel because of late rains.
It rains on the fireworks factory,
rains on the sea, the empires under
the sea, siege machines collapsed in sand,
people reading Proust, every word,
parallel parking, nudge forward, nudge
reverse but somehow no alarm. Some blues singer
plays back what he's just sung, tries again,
hungrier. A long-sequestered love
leaks out in the juicy circumstances
of an accident. She sends another letter
with an alternate destination, a meadow
instead of city, goldfinches on thistle.
The river starts an argument with itself
over rocks some kids drop from the bridge
where weeks ago someone jumped,
another week before he was found
sleeping in his car. Neither does my friend
answer. The copilot's hungover
from his sister's wedding and the plane
ducks the thunderheads. Impeccably
the insects groom themselves, each foreleg

ending with what looks like a mascara brush.
Your eyes go on being the sky's,
beautiful sentiments set off to oblivion
while across town the new opera's booed.
You walk among the racks of dresses absently
clattering the hangers. So many blues.

These End-Stopped Affairs

Honestly, ouch, beauty is.
Alarming when you finally looked at me,
I had been so used to your profile, having two eyes and a whole mouth
        to deal with—
Alarm!
No doubt trees express alarm differently than people
who have more in common with ocelot and jerboa
but one morning every ginkgo whammo drops its leaves.
Both in cause and consequence—alarm.
Alarm in drudgery, alarm in panache.
In the beginning everything was smashed into a ball
then the ball got fuzzy and rolled down a hill
and turned out to be three baby foxes.
Then a small community sprang up around the caldera, mostly jewelers.
A river sticks its finger down its throat—presto, another river.
My friend says, Put the letters in the trash.
Now.
I didn't do a very good job lashing myself to the mast.
It's neurological I feel like I've been shouting all my life.
Everyone's pretty sick of me shouting.
Then some.
What movie is it where they're watching the guy drown under ice
        then we get his point of view and feel worse for them and their
        insignificant struggles?
In the beginning then .0000017 seconds later—alarm.
To look deep into the sky is to look back in time
but to look into your eyes is to see myself
simultaneously baby and old man
oscillating wildly between the poles
of opera and hootenanny.
We walked by the sea that couldn't calm down.
Some birds were going crazy.
We had to pry lunch from its shell.

Internal combustion took you someplace vivid
while I got blurrier and blurrier.
You were expecting and scared me sharing the revolving door.
You were nearly killed putting up Xmas decorations.
I don't know who I is anymore.
I called you from the frozen night to unnumb.
You had the ability to detect very diffuse scents
but you'd die if you stopped swimming.
You went up the chimney and joined the clouds.
You undeleted me.
You got the letters out of the trash.
I went on believing in you without any proof
but what's the challenge in believing what can be proved?
Someone died, you went away or I did, turning the golden faucets in
        the strange restroom.
10 seconds it takes a cheetah to reach 45 miles per hour.
You'd start an argument about anything, the wallpaper, then be the
        little punished boy locked in the basement by his mother again
        then you'd stop shaving and try to learn how to be alone and
        unafraid, hours trying to sleep without prescription.
You meaning me, me meaning who?
He tried out electric basses all afternoon
but by evening there it was again—the vision of her fucking someone
        else.
I wanted more from you meaning you and more meaning more.
A bunch of crows decided which tree
to become one darkness in.
The shadow of the earth takes a bite of the moon then spits it out.
You were so afraid of spiders, I had to get rid of one of my shirts.
I didn't make a pass at your sister even years later at the airport bar.
I was a good glacier.
Then one day you can't connect a K to an O in your own handwriting.
Possibly otherwise
is only the result of the faulty apparatus used to examine the past.
It turns out no easier to be a butterfly than a Chinese emperor.
Who *are* these people?

We know what you're going through, sing the sirens.

I did hallucinogens for corroboration,

skydiving for a tranquilizer.

Your author never finished you off, a sudden malady did him in first.

A cheep emerged, then a whole bird.

Even the wind was pleated.

The door was painted to look like it was already open on a garden when
       what was behind it were dumpsters.

Will be can't be must don't never if you if you

gaping hole in my chest or what?

You spin clockwise above the equator, counterclockwise below.

You are a five-foot nerve.

You are made of bent coat hangers, honey, gravel, epoxy and handstands.

I am made of lying on the floor, the same song on repeat.

Then you are falling asleep.

More people are killed by champagne corks than spider bites.

Everything carries explosion in itself, is carried by, which comes out as
       stridulation, swimming up waterfalls, Abstract Expressionism,
       sapphires.

We are perforated.

Then one of those alarm clocks that incrementally increases the
       volume—Vivaldi again—

so you can catch your ride.

You're a reindeer, you say, hardly opening your eyes.

Elemental

The night doesn't summarize the day.
The spark has its say over the fire.
Dearheart, why are you crying?
Already you're in the air.

Quiet doesn't summarize the song
which can't go on for long,
song found inside us feral and hot.
Dearheart, why are you crying?
We're sparks.

Walked into the burning woods and burning
walked into me. One day we'll wade
into the sea and see. You're coming
won't summarize your leaving

nor waking sleep, sleep our dreams,
fireflies over wet grass, ice
settling in an abandoned glass. Winter
can't summarize that summer, your body

in my hands won't summarized be
by your body far from me.
Already you're in the air
and my hands are nowhere,

my dreams mostly water.
This end won't summarize our forever.
Some things can be fixed by fire,
some not. Dearheart, already we're air.

2

Flamenco

The sexual gasps coming from the garden shed
of my friends turning twenty, tipsy
droll joke of my friends turning thirty, lost
car keys even with tied-to-them a silly whistle
turning forty, bullshit about September
the most passionate month fifty, bird-watching
nap my friends sixty, turning empty chair
at card-club oh my friends turning, turning
while I remain unchanged, a peach pit,
still assisting an ant with a stick,
tapping a peanut to signal a squirrel,
a collection of eternal accidents
while the body, without pity, shrinks,
expands, noises coming from it like
trapped rabbits, sometimes muffled
xylophone, its liquids fermenting,
drunk on itself, dance just foot slams,
painting just spray and spill, brain commanding
its grit to become ruby, won't, tears amniotic,
incinerated dust then an oblivious nephew
given my watch in a velvet sack,
my ghost eating mulberries in a tree,
still stained, my tyrannosaurus skull still
trying to poke through a mouse hole in the cosmos.

Song

The mind is no evergreen steadily green
among extremes of temperature, it's more squid
flushed with mood, one second smoochy, next
a puff of opaque ick. Oh, flying off the handle,
oh, orgasm, ice-cream headache, oh one way
then quick reversal like foot soldiers who
do not grasp the abstract concepts
that dragooned them to this field
to assault a brother who just wants like them
to see his squeeze again at harvest time
when the air is full of chaff and buzz and moo.
Oh, youth, sings the older sister, second
note lower than the first and a little
to the side trying to calm her can't-be-done-
therefore-I'll-do-it kid sibling. The choreographer
grabs one end, the philosopher the other
thus the couch is moved from one wall to another
just as theory and practice must adroitly co-
ordinate to get a thing done. Too much practice:
the couch just flies around the stage; too much
theory: couch is just an idea negating its supportive
purpose for slouching when one is tuckered out
from either/or and groans. And groans the river
to the sea, the dog to her fleas, all things,
the known and unknown groan, it is the hocus-
pocus gnosis of this world.

Wolfspeak

It's like Blueberry saying she's a lake
and all people can do is dump in her
a busted four-door.
No, it's like you spend half your life kicking
the supports out from under stuff
to prove everything can float
and even though everything collapses,
So far, you say, so far.
No, it's like you're repeating yourself
which is actually a bad copy of someone else
saying the world's a dream
of someone who's eaten nothing
but praying mantises for weeks.
No, the world's a dream
of someone eating the world
then throwing half away because
a banquet's not a banquet unless half's thrown away.
Well maybe but also it's like you're digging
and you hear screaming
then thank god you just missed the baby rabbits!
Well, if you're going to bring god in,
it's like god wanted to hide you
only you got tired of waiting to be found
so you leapt into the garage light
and said Here I am
which scared the mignon out of everyone
because you are a wolf.
You know the deal.
How everything laces up.
You have a halo.
Sometimes you trot into town to drink from swimming pools
even though you know it's bad for you.
People misunderstand your smile.

Also lakes
and the inner flotation of all things.
The most misunderstood airplane
is a coffin.
Nothing is ever lost.
You can't forget where you are
when you're never anywhere
like a star. The star's coloring book
is just like yours: the universe.
Almost none of the black crayon left.
People misunderstand black crayons
but put a baby rabbit in their mitts,
they'll feel immense panic.
Maybe not right away
but soon and forever.

Tangle

I have been the best man in a blizzard.

I know why they put seashells around the baby corpse
a million years ago.

I made the cotton candy bloody.
I've been wounded by kite string,
by a letter from Nico in a helpful way.

The sea is never angry when it finds me.
It knows my suicides are snowflakes.

The quickest part always corresponds to the human heart.
Ditto the darkest parts of the forest.
Keats went there.

When he was dying he said he felt flowers already growing over him
but possibly it was the wallpaper on the ceiling.
Is no one allowed to wear the cape of eyes and ears
since the angel did? I think not.

Hello, we are neon.

The small scrawl at the end of a letter.
Trees with holes in them for families of owls.

What was your worst breakup?
It hurts to find a new vanishing point.

But don't despair.
There are designs that seem like chaos
only because you're too close.

The Past

Ouch a little was the unremote spring
band-aid ripped off then thank-you moan
summered in your hair I tried to get
nearer or run away over the phrenological
gravel if I dared there was a blue scare
and red surge meaningful because we were
on a roof and some birds without answering
their names felt like fabric slipping
through the hand I thought you said death-
not depth-perception this was his last
painting the gallery owner said in sand
later it was a constant reckoning of sand
beach each to each in exegesis of never
a discourse that delivers over time
a clearer more finalized representation
we started laughing people were having
sex next door vociferously then had some
ourselves my mail was being held
you were female of every zip source
a story gone through many morning napkins
of night the tomato starts guitar fights
walking with the ice chest over roots
the shoulder whining Use the other
unless very loud in ant-ese the ants
won't turn around they are time
some clothes on some clothes off
oval frames where the straight-faced
dead to put and on the table a book
of monkey faces dance studio anguish
stillness like a lightbulb and tadpoling
waist pillow smooch of cloudbreak
if we have wind enough in mind every harbor
seems favorable is not what Coleridge wrote

nectarines Cézanne the throat presence
of ancient Greece in the vinaigrette
by the strophe anti-strophe un-pain-avoiding
sea dawn's compass-drawn triangles poetry
of the known driving through the unknown's
car-wash coming out polished dead bugs
gone from the windshield still got to put
gas in Bucko a sign saying other way
did you remember to say thank you
she comes back a completely different person
in the same mind-altering skirt although
now she's 27 instead of 16 a larger
size it was a musical approximation
by lurches and splashes leaps and collapses
memory installs the past you may be forgiven
for being confounded but not forgotten
fording a breeze of month-long
afternoon the waitress seemed increasingly
perturbed as I increasingly overtipped
which only made the drinks cost more
undrunkenness put its hermeneutic
in the mix then thought Oh what the heck
the planets were in a mood the flowers
splashed and resplashed in the splash machine
the father fell over at the zoo holding
his son up to see the polar bear cracking
his head I was close enough to do nothing
until unshaded and reshaded I did the boy's
eyes to check pupil dilation okay
I had some explaining you were un-able
meanwhile the rustification process
had entered from the wings on August
oxidations irritating to buy a present
for people not known yet when the bride comes
down the aisle meringued on the not-arm
of the dead father/friend you choke up

choke up you were told on the bat you
always like to be up first to fight
against your feelings becoming manageable
it was funny the X's and O's on coach's
clipboard meant very different than
those ending the text message not much
longer so longing kicks in like one
of those water taffy stretchers in the shops
on the Jersey boardwalk called I think
a mangle must have been fifty hooks
and eyes and frogs holding you in still
it didn't slow us down totem pole of owls
crazy quilt on one side just sleepy
cotton cumulus on the other stitched
together by seasick stars it meant
a labor had been loved the mirror splashed
too the scars shown a song we waited for
the taxi answered the lady in Nut Palace
saying We need to fatten you up you look
like Fred Astaire I'd rather Beckett
the tree wasn't even a tree just a black
cutout and nothing else on stage
now that's skinny the dog used only bark-
geometry when he needed calculus
to unwind his leash you patted the cushion
and looked at me like a photograph
of an avalanche I was glad I wasn't
a tree cutout and there wasn't a war
for a while the chore was laundry
the poor there was a lot undissolved
by the storm but moved about then stopped
as if in freeze tag the fun being
frozen in funny position even collapsing
I'm not sure why maybe I am and the fog
and gone the lilacs until next year we
won't be here there elsewhere already

like a whistle's purpose and the bones
to hold out the hand How are you
It's been too long then zoom off
is carried the jaywalking feather
on the sunburned shoulders of the sea.

Infinitive Ode

To see the pile of skulls Cézanne sketched
as practice for his painting of hovering peaches.
To see the hovering not as inept perspective.
To see in the pantomime of invalids

the corps de ballet. The ocean waits patiently,
I used to think I'd never drown.
To see my hand on fire touching your breast,
to gain altitude so fast the nose bleeds

and the nosebleed scarlet as your kiss.
To be lucky to be man and woman,
not tar paper and a giraffe, not paper clip
and race car. The man meeting the woman

getting off her train is called To Leap Magnolias.
The woman waiting for the man at the hotel bar
is called To Be a Thief of Fire. Hello, waterfall.
Hello, cricket, your singing is bigger than the house.

To take two bites and be full
and to be utterly insatiable.
One must have a mind of many breezes
to fly a kite, to be a kite tangled

in the high-tension wires like an ideogram—
what does it say? A sword pierces a cloud
like a smile blown from a face.
To be the busted umbrella scuttled

down the storm-addled street.
The radio goes further and further back,
past Lou Reed, past the Kingston Trio
and there it is: the blues.

To be purified by the memory
of touching the arch of your foot.
Fragile are the bones of a bat.
Fragile even the suspension bridge.

To preserve the dream under the tongue
all day, not garbling a word. To wash
with cold water. All the way to the ground
the sky comes, just lying down we're flying.

Easy as Falling Down Stairs

To always be in motion there is no choice
even for the mountain and its frigid
cousins floating on the oceans that even sluggish
seethe and moan and laugh out loud at their own
jokes. How *like the human heart* can be said of
pert near everything, pint of fizz, punching
bag because all moves: the mouse, the house,
the pelt of moon corresponding to the seas
(see above) (now get back here) of mood,
sadness heaving kelp at the sunken city's
face, gladness somersaulting from the eaves
like a kid's drawing of a snowflake. No matter
how stalled I seem, some crank in me
tightens the whirly-spring each time I see
your face so thank you for aiming it
my way, all this flashing like polished
brass, lightning, powder, step on the gas,
whoosh we're halfway through our lives,
fish markets flying by, Connecticut,
glut then scarcity, hurried haircuts,
smell of pencils sharpened, striving,
falling short, surviving because we ducked
or somehow got enough shut-eye even though
inside the hotel wall loud leaks. I love
to watch the youthful flush drub your cheeks
in your galloping dream. Maybe even
death will be a replenishment. Who knows?
Who has the time, let's go, the unknown's
display of emeralds closes in an hour,
the fireworks' formula has changed, will we
ever see that tangerine blue again, factory
boarded up then turned into bowling lanes.

Undertow

People looking at the sea,
makes them feel less terrible about themselves,
the sea's behaving abominably,
seems never satisfied,
what it throws away it dashes down
then wants back, yanks back.
Comparatively, thinks one vice president,
what are my frauds but nudged along
misunderstandings already there?
I can't believe I ever worried
about my betrayals, thinks the analyst
benefiting facially from the sea's raged-up mist.
Obviously I'm not the only one suffering
an identity crisis knows the boy
who wants to be a lawyer no more.
Nothing can stay long, cogitates the dog,
so maybe a life of fetch is not a wasted life.
And the sea heaves and cleaves and seethes,
shoots snot out, goes to bed only to wake
shouting in the mansion of the night, pacing,
pacing, making tea then spilling it,
sudden out-loud laughter snort, Oh what the
hell, I probably drove myself crazy
thinks the sea, kissing all those strangers,
forgiving them no matter what, liars
in confession, vomiters of plastics
and fossil fuels but what a stricken
elixir I've become even to my becalmed depths,
while through its head swim a million
fishes seemingly made of light
eating each other.

Ephemerides

Trying not to let the radiance of the cosmos
overwhelm any normal cognitive function,
the hope was the wedding would be over
before the storm hit the Palisades, already

some specks in an in-law whorl. The one
who felt like a goat tied to a stake
watched a red arm cross the table
of the radar map. Something raw

and meatlike about the corsages.
Gilgamesh saying no to the goddess
to disastrous aftereffect, facedown,
spread open on the nightstand but Darcy

finally making his move in 20 pages
on the other side of the bed.
There's no way to tell what goes on
inside a person's head although

a series of probes during brain surgery
indicates locales like how in one bar
everyone throws darts and in another
tries to talk. Love is always impossible.

So's getting out of bed, cowboy.
One morning the parakeet was just lying
on the cage floor so she left town
the next day for good. Spring Beauties

stampeding over the graves, quicklings
of gum-foil scuttling down the gutters.
They're married now, the one whose parents
hadn't shared a time zone for years

and the one who would always have paint
under his fingernails. They were part
of the world that flew apart in every direction
yet came together to form little knots

sometimes called Everlasting, sometimes
Feverwort.

Vacationland

I dreamt I was somewhere else
and woke up there. Huge cables
hung above me like someone else's ideas
of guilt, they could get you somewhere
but in another season. A dog I knew
trotted by, ignoring me for other rabbits.
Astral bodies bickered and kissed in secret
corridors of the wrestling heat while I searched
for a familiar beverage among the dislocated
fruit swirls and waved at a girl on a balcony
who seemed trapped but perfectly happy,
the blast of air-conditioning behind her
ready for her to return to hibernation.
How extraordinary that other people
even exist! puns stenciled
across their chests, waddling
inflatables to the beach, paying
way too much for water, meaty, explodable,
joyous as weeds. It's an odd job
we have anyway, avoiding each other
and constantly meeting again,
comparing notes on sleeplessness,
a reading list of phantoms,
the gummy mutter of cell phones
way past dawn. I'm sorry
for your loss, at least I would be
given the opportunity. The same thing
happened once to me or someone like me
or will. The higher you get, the more
the details point away from the hirsute
occasion—the marmot's golden teeth,
the divorcées playing volleyball on the beach—
to a cracked sheet of rock. Sorry

to be such an airhead downer. Out there
somewhere is the end of everything
but only the mountains are comfortable
with the idea. The rest of us paddle,
paddle between what we can't get
away from and where we don't want to go.

Music Was My Education

I thought I had a window seat
but it was middle all the way.
I wasn't hurting anyone, just
minding my own business which I have none,
makes me purer, easier to blend in
with the cloud-crowd
and the murmurers of lost love's name.
Talk with a girl who knew a lot about invisible matters,
some philosopher had rapt her.
Sounded like harassment to me,
no antidote for that anecdote.
Then in a dream I realize my own beautiful darling
was truly gone to me
then it was lutes galore.
We were over the sea by then,
would be forever.

Full-Time at the Cyclotron

The dog smelling what-uck on a pole,
suddenly I know I'll be an awful,
dim and recognizable character
in my ex-wife's next novel. How sudden
is such a thought? Faster than curtains thrown
back on a world spackled with snow?
Where did summer go, cue the violins?
Bus seems slow while on it, quick when missed.
Pale being, you slip through minute's netting
like minnows over a chessboard. Checkmate.
How did this red get here? I wonder if
de Kooning thought handed a loaded brush
for his last painting. Oh well, whoosh.

Articles of Faith

I used to like Nicole Kidman
now I like Kirsten Dunst.
Jennifer Aniston is a schmuck
but Brad's sure a rotter
even if I was the only one who liked him in *Troy*
he had the Achillean pout right.
I much prefer the *Creature from the Black Lagoon*'s environmental warning
to the *Invisible Man*'s exploration of neurosis
although in the update with Kevin Bacon
I like the nudity.
When it says at the bottom in small print
language, gore and nudity
I like that
but the *Sisterhood of the Traveling Pants*
made me cry on an airplane,
got to be from lack of cabin pressure.
Grown men should not wear shorts in airports
unless they are baggage handlers.
Bearded men should never play the flute.
Most heavy metal music is anger over repressed homoerotic urges
is the sort of idea that got me beat up in high school.
There is nothing sadder than a leaf
falling from a tree then catching an updraft higher than the tree
then getting stuck in a gutter.
Symbolism is highly suspicious because it can't be helped.
There is always something you can never touch, never have
but there it is, right in front of you.
The opposite is also true.
Even though the bells are ringing
your glissando is private.
Truth labors to keep up with the tabloids.
Every word is a euphemism.
Every accident is organized by a secret system

and you're telling me life isn't personal?

The starfish disgorges its stomach to devour its prey.

A network of deceptions festoons the cortege.

An X-Acto knife cuts a kingfisher from an oil company ad.

In the beginning the divine creator wrote 999 words and created
       999 demigods to translate each word into 999 words and 999
       angels to translate each translated word into 999 words and
       999 exalted priests to translate each translated word of the
       translated words into 999 words and we are an error in the
       transcription of one of those words.

Vows exchanged in an aerodrome.

Ovals without consequence.

Masterpiece wrapping paper.

The hurricane makes of homes exploded brains.

Central Intelligence Agency.

The early explorers were extremely agitated men, antisocial, violent,
       prone to drink.

Demons walk the earth.

Says so on a T-shirt.

We are born defenseless.

It's a miracle.

The True Apology Takes Years

The true apology takes years.
Terrible dry eyes!
The tree rings grow closer and closer together
but the nail is swallowed.
Great heaps of rubble are moved up and down the shore.
Finally a dance is performed to complete the forgiveness,
stamping out small fires,
the whole palladium decorated with thistles
like the last twenty pages of a Victorian novel.
Now that your hunger is gone you're welcome to the banquet.
Many immense things are hidden from us
but not too many.
Shutters thrown open on the courtyard
where ghost horses come to drink at the ancient fountain.
Children in heavy clogs chasing hoops.
An old man doesn't want to take his secret
of adhering gold leaf to wood to this grave.
Already the grave is burnished gold,
embossed with peacocks.
He has not spoken to his son for how many years?
Not since the political arguments really about
his wife, the mother dying when the lemons were in blossom.
How neither son nor father could accept it no matter
the other insisting. Screaming.
There is an old trail that goes to the cliffs,
a memory of watching ships
and the weather coming in.
The son now owns a field of clover
for bees in Vermont.
Hundreds cover his bare skin
like a piano sonata
and he does not flinch.
How long can a voice be kept in a golden fluid?

What will his father make of the jars of honey?
It is almost time.
The musicians begin buzzing,
a hand is raised, a foot slides forward.

The Fox

Remember trying to feed the fox?
She said five feet is close enough.
Throw me something or put it on the ground
and go away. She favored a front paw.
You sat down. She sat down
so everything stopped, a wheel ceased
squeaking, firecracker caught open-
mouthed, the children froze around
the hospital bed, a minor chord sustained
who knows how, innumerable rain-
drops suspended midair becoming
conscious of their fate to be dashed down,
a song formed wholly at once just as wholly
vanished, phosphenes, starworks, dustshop
each must blunder off to in our time,
freed of love, without fuss, our orders
sketchy at best. The problem isn't having two hearts
or a ghost marriage or their voice
changing so they'd have to leave the chorus.
One day, the fox doesn't show.
That's as close as you'll ever get
but she's already figured out
how to appear in your dreams, just
not yet, not until you've stopped
being nervous at twilight. Debussy,
when he felt his opera going nowhere,
let it.

After My Own Heart

Perfect citadel wherever an ant is.

Today I touched a blind man
forward onto the escalator.
Tomorrow my ticket will still be good.

Some laughter falls from its bouquet.
Some tears too.

The scar in my forehead is almost gone
and July is almost gone,
month I fell in love in,
no big surprise, none bigger.

And numerously.

Something is always tumbling
down the steps in my chest
carrying a birthday cake.
I want what I get.

I like to think of you busy,
maybe washing parsley
and I am completely forgotten.

Nothing of the pantomime, even shadows
sometimes sit with their heads in their hands.

The train stops for a while under the bay.
Blinks.
Then we rise back into the messages,
prodigal, disremembered.

I always search for your face
even when I look straight out
at the fog over the sea
and the fog over the sea
becomes my face.

Have you noticed how ants meet?
Their language single molecules exchanged,
that's why they keep so clean.
They say Here and Hello.
They say Found and How far.

They touch each other all over.

Scenes from the Crystal World

That Ravel's "Bolero" was used in the naked
Bo Derek seduction scene in *10*
and the pageant buildup to the monster-slaughter
in *Conan the Barbarian* should tell us
something of our predicament. The barbarian
became the Golden State's governor
and the crocus will spell out nothing
even though they were planted to.
So much easier to pass a law
than repeal one, to ring out the bells
than get the ring back in.
The mind must undergo some change
the charts should show in shifting color,
a film of blue over the red crenulations
producing a leafiness, sweet rustle
in the understory. Some impurities
make water clearer. I couldn't even
open my garage door this morning
because of the ice and other aspects
of the quotidian duly noted: canceled
choir practice, outages. Most
of it doesn't match up but good luck
surviving the holidays. The man who
usually wins the fight is the first
to know he's in one, said the wise guy
before sucker-punching me, a cousin
of distant remove on the bride's side
I do believe. When you live in a world
of crystal and fall, you just become
more crystal but once you hold a wren,
window-bonked unconscious, in your hand,
its revival, you'll never be the same again.
It weighs almost nothing then, sudden
flutter, less.

Optimistic Poem

You expected an affordable daydream
but got an unhinged psalm. Oh well,
you expected an early spring, no less
than you, hell, everyone deserves, vexed

as we are with these frizzled oscillations,
the motor hardly turning over, the last
of our fathers lifeless on the left side,
a rowboat slosh in his voice. But throw back

your shot glass of tears, my dear, wink
into the mirror: you're still here after all.
Love floats its bone in the throat,
sometimes it hurts to swallow. The moon,

once so full of itself, now spills
a richer, more tipsy eclipse upon
the boondocks, kidnapped kids resurfacing
in convenience stores across this fair land,

tattooed but elfin still with a new knowledge
of mankind. Some definitions chip away but others,
some fulsome, some frisky, some calm
come forth to take up neglected objects,

direct and indirect both so the healing
may commence reconnecting us, what
we've been alarmed wouldn't be freely
dispensed but turns out already lurking

inside us like that tiny, liquid-filled orb
inside a golf ball, where god is or the beginning,
that first density, first word we learned
to read. In my case it was *look*.

Late Valentine

We weren't exactly children again,
too many divorces, too many blood panels,
but your leaning into me was a sleeping bird.
Sure, there was no way to be careful enough,
even lightning can go wrong but when the smoke
blows off, we can admire the work the fire's done
ironing out the wrinkles in favor of newer ones,
ashy furrows like the folds in the brain
that signal the switchbacks and reversals
of our thought and just as brief. Your lips
were song, your hair everywhere.
Oh unknowable, fidgeting self, how little
bother you were then, no more
than a tangerine rind. Oh unknowable
other, how I loved your smell.

Happy Zero-th Birthday, Gideon

Welcome, baby. This is the upside-down
world of singing metal ornaments
in the tangle breeze. I can see by my shadow
how you see me, astray as an electrocuted
squirrel, lights out in this part of the whorl,
the chorus rushing around mouths unstoppered
with Ohs. You won't always be such a tiny
out-of-control blob under towering out-
of-control blobs like trees fixed to the sky
when the ground drops away, hovering lit-up
like kissing nervous systems. Some weird shit
goes down here, baby, but soon your motor skills
will save you from rolling into the river
or throwing yourself from the bridge
although that will primarily be the power
of self-preservation that is with you
even now, working in your willingness
to suckle. Basically, there's the nipple
then everything else. Baby, that will change
somewhat but the river will always be there
waiting in freeze, hurrying in thaw
like a lover you can never fully have
no matter you're soaked and muddy, shivering
gasping on the bank or staring into her depths
that seem both still and boiling over.
Maybe a turtle on a log will know something else
but the river will tell you you can start anew
and that everything is ruined and everyone
lied to you and you are free and must go back
to make things right you can't go back
you're already dust you'll live forever,
the whole contradictory mess. Maybe your first
friend will be lost to a flu. There's

nothing you can do but people love you.
Maybe your leg is broken in six places
or you can name every wildflower left
or when you say Hello, the cliff
smacks it right back in your face
and you have a halo
and a robot of gold.
What do I know?
It won't even be the same river.

Non-Apologia

Maybe poetry is all just artifice,
devices, hoax, *blood* only there
to rhyme with *mud*, signs wandering off
from that picnic blanket where once
the word lounged with the naked girl
of meaning for Manet to paint. Now
we think we're not mistaking
the escaped squid for the cloud of ink
but the squid keeps coming back
in its miraculous mood-alterable skin
just as words never stop escaping back
into meaning, word *electric*, word
cardiovascular, falling short, sure,
word *derriere* falling short of the actual
ass you'd lief fondle instead
of reading and writing about squid.
Don't we love words too for themselves,
how *liquid* is almost *squid*
but worry about *laughter* in *slaughter?*
It's always one way *and* the other.
Poetry paints nothing but it splashes
color, flushed, swooning, echolocating
and often associated with flight
as in Keats's *viewless wings of Poesy,*
a weird statement. The wings can't see?
Are invisible like Wonder Woman's plane?
Poetry is a good provider of the strange.
A hubcap waggle to me conviction.
No time for the present.
Beep ping dragon machine.
Perhaps even more than nonnative speakers,
poetry delights if you want not
the humdrum quotidian gist,

rather a sudden brain-spinning love
for a stranger wearing a coral necklace like the sea.
Even spiders sing. We all are arpeggios
make that archipelagoes but oh, the butter
of your utterance unbanishing me
from the island of myself. Poetry is dandy
at supplying figurative language
which some find frustrating and evasive.
Why doesn't he just say outright
he wants to kiss her instead of going on
about butter? Well, screw you, to be sick
of metaphor is to be sick of the otherness
of life, in life which is like preferring
masturbating to the team sport or forms
without their depth-giving shadows.
A thing is never only itself.
Sometimes it rhymes.
Soon shadows are all that's left,
that's why poetry is about death.

Flamenco

Live as if you have nothing,
says the sailboat. Are you kidding,
says the snail, can't you see we'd better
hurry? Someone walks into a bakery,
shakes his head at the cakes then leaves,
goes back to the thing he's making
with a thousand lightbulbs.
It's complicated. It doesn't need to be,
says the quadratic equation sick of itself.
Do you realize what time it is? scolds
a speck of dust. A few formalities
exchanged between the lion and her prey.
Finish the bottle, even the worm
with a toast to self-extermination.
I mean determination *hic.*
A yellow plastic bag, no one can wrestle it
to the ground, first it's fire then famine
then the secret of eternal youth.
You could try clapping at the end of every line,
stomping your foot. A day at the seashore
might do you some good, the bull-stampeding
waves. I had no choice, complains the rain.
Did you even want one? answers the river.
Oh dead friend still on my answering machine!

3

Changing Genres

I was satisfied with haiku until I met you,
jar of octopus, cuckoo's cry, 5-7-5,
but now I want a Russian novel,
a 50-page description of you sleeping,
another 75 of what you think staring out
a window. I don't care about the plot
although I suppose there will have to be one,
the usual separation of the lovers, turbulent
seas, danger of decommission in spite
of constant war, time in gulps and glitches
passing, squibs of threnody, a fallen nest,
speckled eggs somehow uncrushed, the sled
outracing the wolves on the steppes, the huge
glittering ball where all that matters
is a kiss at the end of a dark hall.
At dawn the officers ride back to the garrison,
one without a glove, the entire last chapter
about a necklace that couldn't be worn
inherited by a great-niece
along with the love letters bound in silk.

Is This Why Love Almost Rhymes with Dumb?

In love there's many obstacles
like in summer trying to protect an icicle,
the ship a wreck, the surf a debacle,
so sometimes love seems to deserve distain
like tarnish brought on by rain,
the rain of course standing in for tears,
all the bitterness and self-accusing fears
of other relationships fucked-up for years.
The fissures open in the dull afternoon hours
but it's time to throw away those wilted flowers,
get some air, ride a bike, take a shower.
When we split, friends tell us to feel relieved,
a message we no better receive
than wanting to stay in the bar but told to leave.
Now the head hurts like a mean monkey,
worries about getting old, no money,
wanting right now to be buried like a pharaoh in honey.
Let's not drag this all out another time,
even at midnight the bells know when to stop their chime,
even given the dictates of rhyme
that make outcomes so predictable, fated,
you'd think we'd all be more jaded
and not feel so overcome, overrun, raided.
But, darling, does it have to be so?
Take those coupling hawks which every which way go,
one dive-bombing, one on thermals rising slow
yet tumbling together they won't separate.
Admit it, you're forever my mate,
at each dawn alarm and no matter how hurryingly late,
after sunset for an hour or two
the world always seems to glow more you.
Maybe the glue won't waggle completely loose,
my arms still churn me through the pool,

everyone knows I've always been a fool.
Maybe I'll have a ham and cheese sandwich
or skip lunch altogether hardly matters which
if only I could breathe without a hitch.
I could become nothing but a shadow
or try to learn to take it slow
and not into panic everything throw,
sit for a week with uncrazy expectations,
not be seasick on seesaw contradictory revelations,
write nothing new, just make emendations,
aim for the perfect footnote,
come up with one good joke,
stop sinking like uranium but like goose-feather float.
We still love each other, always will
even though sometimes the other we half want to kill.
Two things at least are certain: there's no pill
and of you I'll never get my fill.

Three Weeks from Two Days Ago

Waiting is the moon, waiting the groom
in the little boy. The red minute waits
in the white afternoon, the dream in the daylit
consciousness. Is god what's waiting

to hear back, we the message sent out
into the void? You wait for something to appear
but in most cases the opposite is true,
wait long enough it's all gone, the year's

preparatory nubs on the weeping pussy willow,
pregnant woman in the airport taxi queue
reading a book of names. Alphabet
to be rearranged into the spelling of your name

just as you rearranged me so I thought
let's have lunch in a tree, winter already
spring, bells to drink champagne from.
I couldn't wait to see you again

so tried to warp space-time
with sexual energy alone, what a joke,
especially over the phone, sorry.
Slower the shorter days go, the pool

closed a month ago, goldfinches gone
from the coneflowers, coneflowers
brown bent low, hardly any need to mow,
it's cold, it snows, just a few crab apples

left on the bare tree to ferment so spring
returning waxwings can get drunk enough
to almost touch as I am almost touching you
not wanting to wait.

Alternating Current

Throbbing is the sunflower,
throbbing is the sea, one two three
periods in a row, no, not periods,
ellipsis and on and on the locusts go.
Silly boy scrubbing at a spot, solar eclipse
projecting half-bitten dot in the pinholed box.
And throbbing is the head upon the breast,
throbbing the knot inside the chest
so I can hardly say your name. Trains
rattle down by the river, the finger
with its sliver throbs, the first
Monday of every month, Grandmother polished
the silver. Is life just intervals of pulses,
ripples spreading on a lake
from where the rock was tossed? Do not
forsake me darling though we be carried off.
Every instance has its day and night,
every inkling is full of blinks,
the power going on and off so fast
we can hardly think until here comes a storm,
poor dog scuttled under the bed, poor dream
we recall almost not at all no matter
how we cling because throbbing is the sea
and we be torn apart.

Wolf Lying in Snow

Sometimes when I put my hand on my forehead,
that great lament rushing from a storm pipe,
that midnight straining to be daylight,
I don't know what's keeping my peg in its slot.
On the way home I don't explode even though
I'm one of the bad monkeys in the dead deer's eyes.
Remember the theater's promise how just sitting there
would feel like rocketing through outer space
which turned out just dumb? Disappointment's
low moan, consolation's tweet, heroically
tearing a branch from the tree to carry flaming
into the crater and back, back ghost of mother.
Try to stay with me, okay? One more last-sounding
letter from a friend, one more chirpy reply.
Verily the speed freaks heave their flaming
sofa onto the street. Verily the cops'
deus ex battering ram even though the door's
been passed out flat on the front porch
for weeks. Salvage, demolition: depends
on your point of view. No one visits
the woman on the other side of the curtain
probably not recovering either so let's
include her in the conversation even if
she can't answer. Just one floor down
the room's full of balloons. When the hand
is removed from the dummy's spine, it might
stop talking but won't give up on being heard.
Someone still working on numbers in the back
wants to be transparent without first turning
to ash. Good luck. The angel arrives,
the one with pigtails and the sword.
I want you to tell me I won't be alone.
The last time we talked on the phone

you were almost funny about being sick,
voice lurching painkiller-thick,
a joke falling through a hole,
one more rose for the afterlife.

Another Strange Rose for the Afterlife

Broken river, you're not broken after all,
you just dropped your wineglass.

Tattered sky, you're only raining,
get used to it. Not even the brown laurel

is dead, not even the dry things the rushes said
or the little spinning creature, pivot

its smashed innards. Maybe we start out rising
and stay that way, two people really one

shadow in the advancing day, trying
to take the guesswork out of rapture,

hostages of we know not what,
perhaps ourselves or the more perfect other

never seen whose meddling is hardly felt
except as twilight's paw upon one's shoulder

gently prodding us away from each other,
away from the fire toward that clarifying

dark, free as sleep from desire, subject, theme.
But some call remains suspended back there

still rich with ambiguity as a cry of love
sounds like pain and vice versa, both

of which came from you and you caused.

Bay Arena

I could have been doing anything but I wasn't
I was hugging wet clothes into the dryers
that moment in the laundromat when you're most exposed
the leopards have been waiting for in the long grasses
and the coyotes trotting through the dry grasses
and the raptors lying in the long sky.
The tests of the new bomb had obviously gone well
or at least not far better than expected
there were still buildings standing
and human life going into the Marxist bakery
nothing was very good but at least unreified
that would go under in a few years
which is one way you can tell this is the past
no one is covered with sores passed out in a marching band jacket
propped against a parking meter
which still gives you more time than it takes
to put in another nickel for a nickel.
Half of the Oakland hills were about to melt
down private art collections and novel drafts.
Oh what the heck, the house-sitting daughter thinks
nobody believes anything least of all ironic sirens
after loading the cat and dog
goes back for the family photo albums.
Jay was still struggling with Parmenides
how it all comes down to one fragment
a struggle the fragment would win
so he'd never finish his thesis and become
a liability at the bookstore not only for personal hygiene
where a guy waving a jar of Prego extra thick
accusationally came in raving about the New Deal
and everyone looked at me even though no way
was 20th-century US history my area
and the Nobel poet's credit card was refused

and the love of my life who I didn't recognize
because she wasn't in the right body yet
asked me if we were hiring I said no
but it wouldn't hurt to fill out an application
but I was speaking petroglyph and she turned back to fog
and half my body was an orange pushpin in the schedule
and half could still run up the fire road
to the laboratory which wasn't my area either
and back without dying. All the new thinking
was about collision then string then collision again.
Look at this haiku, said Bob.
The particles smash together
and for a nanosecond something exists
that can't any longer.
Bird hiccup.
Scarecrow heart.
Now for the narrative.
Sorry there isn't one
just time making it feel like we're moving
to a point where everything comes together
foreshortened
to vanish and be sorted out
what you overheard in the stockroom that hurt
the herding habits of bats
where all this pink lint is coming from.
Isn't it remarkable world at all holds together?
Let honey be our sustenance
that it is sweet and will not rot.
They can do entire surgeries with light.
The shouting comes from nowhere
and nowhere shouts back.

Instant Recognition between Strangers

Just because we have birds inside us, we don't have to be cages.

But until our names are called, we wait in the dark hall with the coat
trees.

Kafka, Kafka, barks the dog.

The guards forbid kissing the statues lest their spell be broken and they
too feel smothered with joy.

I wish I could have stopped you from getting that tattoo.

I wish I had grown up believing in a god with many arms, but no, just a
lightning bolt.

Dandelion, the sky is burning out again.

They use silver clamps to pluck the bad heart out then install the next.

Maybe a lamb's.

Maybe a crazed motorcyclist's.

Dread is a drum solo because something reaches out and whacks.

Flower house, flower house, no one can live there long.

My Current Favorite Disease

is one where you have sex while asleep
and remember not a jot
thereby making the unconscious hours
most worthy of contemplation hot.
I've heard it's untreatable unlike
lycanthropy and the weepies and all
those lesser verifiable apostasies
we've grown fond of, eating raw cookie dough,
texting old flames snaps of snow,
gusting with mood like a toad in a tornado.
Apparently you come to with a small tattoo,
minor brush burns—that's it,
no inspector this, inspector that,
no imposition of a paradigm shift,
just the sense of walking around unrhymed
which happens all the time reaching
a consensus with nothingness
like a good nihilist. The pop quiz
hardly pops at all. Leaning may be
a learning experience but breaking's
the big test. The leaves speak of oxygenated
diversion, the worm of the body's derision,
the piano turns out to be 88 mousetraps,
an ecstasy of orchestral ouch
in the waking world's alcohol
of ever elsewhere heat, the lawn
left out to rust in the rain again, trains
passing out by the river, hooting
until the morning doves prescribe
their knock-out opiates and I am
re-orphaned, re-kissed, the dancing
not stopped even if everyone's gone,
DJ equipment hauled off, recycling

ported to its redemption, only we
remain to be introduced, the sea
waving us on, boats adrift in the sky.

My Brief Careers

As a doorman I didn't know who wanted in,
who out. As an anesthesiologist, I wanted
every one awake between the rotten heart
cut out and the motorcyclist's installed
to say how it felt. Under the robe,
I wore a holster. I became unafraid
of ladders. I confused the word *career*
with *careen*. I was a walk-on bastard
with three lines dispensed by the second scene.
I mean how one morning you look in the mirror
and there's some foreign, yelping argon
but such tenderness in the world:
people and their guard dogs,
snow smashing its crystals in the lawn,
shushing the crows' ecumenical arguments,
proof of the persistence of the soul
people think you're crazy if you say so
even though they have their own birdbrained
promises tapped out on the night's tins
of rebuffed skepticism.
I believe you get to apologize
maybe twice. See a sunset once.
Death, well, I've lost count.
It turns out a guitar is a lousy oar,
its wand flounders, its head of smoke
can't empty a spit valve. Stabbed
by the sky, stitched up by an unknown
farce. Dad watching me putt into the windmill,
green ball being knocked back.
It's all about timing, how if
you're in the parking lot when she's lost
her keys, you get to kiss her breasts
but if you're in Philadelphia, a star explodes.

That poor piece of music used in a movie
thirty years ago still struggling
to free itself from the seduction of idiots.
I wore a button that said May I help you?
I carried a bucket from the quaking basement.
Who I went to see would soon be dead
and I didn't know how the tape recorder worked.
Who knew pigeons could be so loud?
Is it okay to take on faith the mountains
when all I trample are ant hills?
Is it all right to let the cricket keep me awake?
Autobiography is a story the fireplace
tells to a swimming pool. I'm not sure
what else to embroider in my hankie.
We have to go soon, don't we?
I want to touch everything to be sure.

Demon Cycle

1. Isn't Being Upside Down the Real Game?

Hurt animal, don't you still love the myriad?
Myriad the burning ark, myriad your pop beads
popped. I love the narration of your life
taking longer than my life, more lasting than
its last ashes, a wetter waterfall than its worm.
I love your contaminates, a new red in the network,
new storm huffing to sea. I don't need the sea
to tell me whose sigh I sink back to, I see
the bubbles where it all went down, the surge
when it comes back up, hiccup, drunk licorice
scent of brackish grasses, a faith of guesses.
I don't believe we'll ever truly part, it's just
we can't meet, too magnetic, too repulsive, warps
the day on the wrong warpath but the night,
shot peregrine, keeps splurging in throes.

2. Re-entry

Hello dots on the earth, I thought at first
you might be sickness. Goodbye sky,
aren't you tired of your war with the invisible?
Hello life in the river, I'm not the one
who'll undress you with questions. I'll use
my paws. Hey paws, what trouble have you
unburied now? Do you always have to use
only the red crayon? Hello foliating promise, road
that goes and goes, the closer I get, the more those dots
look like what I should be running from,
measles, a faculty meeting. Why do we say
time's up when it's gone, everything else comes down?
What can you see inside a crow, tree? Church,

go fuck yourself. Šalamun moves among us.
This is radio Iowa City, anyone out there?

3. The Plow Goes Through the World

My friends, the plow goes through the word,
laughter cleaved from slaughter, aster
from disaster, rot from erotic. Smoke comes
from the halo, maybe a benefit of mistranslation.
The morning waking: a slip, a spill, a slur
while the sky gave up its color yet somehow
we find each other. I don't believe in shouts,
don't believe in whispers heavy in fat air
but under dripping umbrellas we fall in love
like giraffes, like sopped skyrockets.
There's never one language for that. Poetry
is always cockeyed, obedient to only other,
what we whisper for, wish to be true, to woo
unto woe. Unsmother me, my darkling divisible
words from other tongues.

4. In the Beginning Was Broken

When did it start? Before the glue
on the crystal, before the man spent
half a life blackening out a name and still
not finished, rust on the iron bridges
that cross from fog to fog. Probably mother
had something to do with it before
she herself was the farewell bride,
crushing a champagne flute, before
the orchids simmered to cinders.
Sleep sky, between my lips, there's no
proper goodbye. On Earth first you must
survive the ants then fill your mouth
with dusks. You must hold yourself

together and apart from the question Why
did it even start? It just did.

5. Happy Hour

How do I love thee, let me count the strays.
I mean lays. Scratch that. Who are you anyway?
What pot of honey is hidden in your snake hole,
what black currants in your eyes? I think
that I shall never see or go fucking crazy if I do
again. Well, crazier. Burned fields of facedown photos,
grand acidic cities, grand tell-alls to ghosts,
glaciers of vodka, how should I know?
Once we were children in a garden.
Buy that? How about we got as far
as the padlock? The beehives were smoked,
your thigh a soap-slide, we both had a family
friend who also cried mountains. Let's not
go back. Let's watch it burn, the thee in me.
Let's flee. Now can I have a drink?

6. Springtime for Snowman

I don't understand the cicadas
in my throat, coal in my chest,
tiny mushrooms called death stars,
scar, scar, scar, all the current theories
declaring the end of meaning although
I don't know what meaning means other
than partaking in the general alarm,
skylark-prickled dawns, inevitability
of causing harm I'd rather not understand.
If my house is on fire, it's no news to me.
If the sinkhole ain't my confidante, I sure
ain't its windmill. No god? No sweat.
No hope? So what. I won't let the ice

on my face be wasted, won't mistake
its melting for tears.

7. ATMOSPHERIC PRESSURE

At the bottom of every beauty,
there's Duchamp saying it's better
with the cracks. Every beauty has its leaks,
handcuffs, busted dolls, wounded owl, tank
of nitrous oxide. How far can anyone get
a finger inside anyone else consensually
anyway? Every beauty hurts but at least
Venus was the single god wounded at Troy
so score one for us. Still, it's a rout.
Beauty, you make me want to shout eat stop
scream cluck rotate help I don't know what
be someone else salt a brownstone wolf-
howl telephone forest full of wriggling
baby Mozart? Reality is some sort of sweet
membrane, lick it right, it rains.

8. HALF-LIFE

In darkness every murmur emerges
from a body of honey. Answers
are snatched from flames, from strange
creatures fed by hand. Music is a mushroom,
an argument between mirrors. Night
condemns us to another life,
that bottom line of the periodic table
where the elements last only nanoseconds.
I'm too sleepy to start over now,
too awake to believe this quicksilver dream.
Please be gentle as an isotope can be,
darling who undresses to disappear.
Nothing breaks down quicker than Dean

Youngium, the last atom before
the first layer of demons.

9. WHAT WOULD THAT LETTER AFTER Z LOOK LIKE

The last question was beyond anything
the class studied. A morning storm
and by afternoon it's summer no more.
I was mistaken about the death of crows,
their shadows never die. I was mistaken
about honeycomb, it's not full of god.
Sometimes the only ending is abrupt but
the man will never finish blackening out
her name. It turns out the burning house
is Byzantium. The breakers rake the beach.
I promise the same promises as hail,
fallen and furious and melting to nothing,
same grit, my love. Goodbye on the wings
of a bur, goodbye. Now it's arithmetic.
Minus plus minus plus minus.

Scarecrow on Fire

Everything is brushed away, off the sleeve,
off the overcoat, huge ensembles of assertions
just jars of buttons spilled, recurring
nightmare of straw on fire, you the scarecrow,
the scare, the crow, totems gone, rubies
flawed, flamingo in hyena's jaws, noble
and lascivious mouth of the gods hovering
then gone, gone the glances, gone moths,
cities of crystal become cities of mud,
centurion and emperor dust, the flower girl,
some of it rises, proof? some of it explodes,
vein in the brain, seedpod poof, maybe
something will grow, another predicament
of bittersweet, dreamfluff milkweed,
declarations of aerosols, vows just sprays
of spit fast evaporate, all of it pulverized
as it hits the seawall, all of it falling snow
on water, flash of flying fish, breach and blow
and sinking, far below creatures of luminous jelly
constellated and darting and baiting each other
like last thoughts before sleep, last neural
sparks coalescing as a face in the dark,
who was she? never enough time to know.

Man Overboard

I would like to thank you for my life,
mother, friends, wife, flirtations,
vexations, crazinesses, those vacations
to Stone Harbor with my dad traipsing up
the beach to the bowling alley for pizza burgers.
Of all that time only remain the sand and me
scrubbed, rolfed, insanely flipped, calmly,
constantly rearranged by typhoon and volleyballers,
Stone Harbor so developed now, expanded, hotels
where dune grass was, the beach that used to be
exclusively the nuns' where I had one
of my first erotic unheaves (in their habits
they surrendered and combating frothy, neo-
platonic surf) is now public though the
bird sanctuary, with its coin-op
binoculars, still has its lenses of cranes
and redwing blackbirds on the trash cans.
I thank that chevron on the wing
for fostering an aesthetic sense that beauty
wasn't extraneous but a part of flying.
Don't fly from me, life, but I know
you must as flying is your modus
operandi in the chest, in the rabbit's nest,
even the subcommittee's neurotransmitters' quest,
liver-spotting, bending until breaking, making
mother's brain unable to remember
me crying un-unusually coming out
during the thunderstorm ago. We loved those
boomers sitting on our Pennsylvania screened porch,
sometimes cruelty zigzagged between us,
she was bigger, sure, could throw me
out of the house during I didn't think
a lot about until years later telling my then-wife

who frightens me saying it explains too much.
Too much life, flashcrack, someone sees
a shark and everyone out of the water.
After a while I wasn't cold or afraid.
I'm sorry mother, you were such a part
of my life I had to fight you off and out,
you wanted other things I don't know what
or how anyone works it out, shouts next door
I think they'll kill each other then
edgy silence maybe they've killed
themselves then the world's restorative vroom,
a new hurry, let's go, class starts
in an hour. Thank you student who
wrote about killing her hamster as a child
I almost cried, the others saying way
too sentimental, me raving, No, it's true
and the one who wrote it turned out
about his father not coming back
from Vietnam for the free-association
assignment: use rhino, mountain,
door, cloud, sword and bituminous
in ten lines or fewer. Thank you fevers,
viral and emotional. Thank you metals,
menial labors, museums of wrecked cars
sprayed off-white, photos of volcanoes,
girls in jog bras lapping me, tea leaves,
trees, lacustrine nights listening
to little genius fucks play Bach
on the radio. Four times their age,
what have I accomplished? Does one take solace
in a life that hardly detonates a flea
or writhe and thrash frantically at
the prevaricating rescue copter?
Thank you Sue, my older sister's friend,
savior who scooped me from the deep end,
gasping, pressed against her beginner breasts,

ruining me with love for an older woman
of sixteen. Later when my heart swelled idio-
pathically, rumorous of failure, I thought
maybe the challenge was not to go out
screaming like being stabbed in the neck
in a fiery ball but with a soft thank-you
nebulizing like the ejecta of an exploded star.
Am I avoiding thanking god? My head
turns mushy when I try to pray so I fear
that god's a product of that mushiness
but thanks anyway, what can it hurt
for whatever part he/she/it/random
particle motion takes in this continuing
life, strife and heights, big box
of crayons with scarlet already snapped,
sky blue nearly a nub, thank you all,
sophomores, deans, drama queens, lustable-afterers,
frustrations, fretting, rose selections,
apology mumblings, art making,
forgetful nonphantoms who I grope
and grill and fleece and ask too much of,
who let me down and fluff me up, ask
why I do these things to myself,
half smirking, half helping while I socket
another million daffodils in the yard.

Delphiniums in a Window Box

Every sunrise, sometimes strangers' eyes.
Not necessarily swans, even crows,
even the evening fusillade of bats.
That place where the creek goes underground,
how many weeks before I see you again?
Stacks of books, every page, character's
rage and poet's strange contraption
of syntax and song, every song
even when there isn't one.
Every thistle, splinter, butterfly
over the drainage ditches. Every stray.
Did you see the meteor shower?
Every question, conversation
even with almost nothing, cricket, cloud,
because of you I'm talking to crickets, clouds,
confiding in a cat. Everyone says
Come to your senses, and I do, of you.
Every touch electric, every taste you,
every smell, even burning sugar, every
cry and laugh. Toothpicked samples
at the farmer's market, every melon,
plum, I come undone, undone.

Winged Purposes

Fly from me does all I would have stay,
the blossoms did not stay, stayed not the frost
in the yellow grass. Every leash snapped,
every contract void, and flying in the crows
lingered but a moment in the graveyard oaks
yet inside me it never stopped so I could not
tell who was chasing, who chased, I could sleep
into afternoon and still wake soaring.
So out come the bats, down spiral swifts
into the chimney, Hey, I'm real, say the dream-
figments then are gone like breath-prints
on a window, handwriting in snow. Whatever
I hold however flies apart, the children skip
into the park come out middle-aged
with children of their own. Your laugh
over the phone, will it ever answer me again?
Too much flying, photons perforating us,
voices hurtling into outer space, Whitman
out past Neptune, Dickinson retreating
yet getting brighter. Remember running
barefoot across hot sand into the sea's
hover, remember my hand as we darted
against the holiday Broadway throng,
silver mannequins in the windows waving,
catching your train just as it was leaving?
Hey, it's real, your face like a comet,
horses coming from the field for morning
oats, insects hitting a screen, the message
nearly impossible to read, obscured by light
because carried by Mercury: I love you,
I'm coming. Sure, what fluttered is now gone,
maybe a smudge left, maybe a delicate under-
feather only then that too, yes, rained away.

And when the flying is flown and the heart's
a useless sliver in a glacier and the gown
hangs still as meat in a locker and eyesight
is dashed-down glass and the mouth rust-
stoppered, will some twinge still pass between us,
still some fledgling pledge?

Teetering Lullaby

Come to rest my darling,
the trees are autumn-twinged,
the ocelot of my mind is out,
would rest in the long grass.

Comes to rest the bus in hydraulic
exhalation, a puppy-scamper wind
finds itself over water and rests,
rest the future fires rushing,
rest the past ash.
                    The heart's
adumbrations of bees may never
cease, not the hopeful hum
or peevish sting but rest I would
my hand upon your breast, sleep I would

above the troposphere. No accounting
for your beauty moving through me
like a branch, a sigh coming from under
the squeaky remnants of the old barn.

Whatever's buried there that once caused
such alarm has come back to forgive,
to apologize for how it all went wrong.

So rest my darling, my daring, the journey's
almost over though I've gone nowhere
and never meant to stay there.

ABOUT THE AUTHOR

Dean Young has received support for his work from the National Endowment for the Arts, the John Simon Guggenheim Memorial Foundation, and the American Academy of Arts and Letters. He is currently the William Livingston Chair of Poetry at the University of Texas, Austin.

Lannan Literary Selections

For two decades Lannan Foundation has supported the
publication and distribution of exceptional literary works.
Copper Canyon Press gratefully acknowledges their support.

LANNAN LITERARY SELECTIONS 2011

Michael Dickman, *Flies*

Laura Kasischke, *Space, in Chains*

Deborah Landau, *The Last Usable Hour*

Valzhyna Mort, *Collected Body*

Dean Young, *Fall Higher*

RECENT LANNAN LITERARY SELECTIONS
FROM COPPER CANYON PRESS

Stephen Dobyns, *Winter's Journey*

David Huerta, *Before Saying Any of the Great Words: Selected Poems*,
translated by Mark Schafer

Sarah Lindsay, *Twigs and Knucklebones*

Heather McHugh, *Upgraded to Serious*

W.S. Merwin, *Migration: New & Selected Poems*

Taha Muhammad Ali, *So What: New & Selected Poems, 1971–2005*,
translated by Peter Cole, Yahya Hijazi, and Gabriel Levin

Travis Nichols, *See Me Improving*

Lucia Perillo, *Inseminating the Elephant*

James Richardson, *By the Numbers*

Ruth Stone, *In the Next Galaxy*

John Taggart, *Is Music: Selected Poems*

Jean Valentine, *Break the Glass*

C.D. Wright, *One Big Self: An Investigation*

For a complete list of Lannan Literary Selections from
Copper Canyon Press, please visit Partners on our Web site:
www.coppercanyonpress.org

Since 1972, Copper Canyon Press has fostered the work of emerging, established, and world-renowned poets for an expanding audience. The Press thrives with the generous patronage of readers, writers, booksellers, librarians, teachers, students, and funders — everyone who shares the belief that poetry is vital to language and living.

Copper Canyon Press gratefully acknowledges board member

JIM WICKWIRE

in honor of his many years of service to poetry and independent publishing.

Major support has been provided by:

Amazon.com

Anonymous

Beroz Ferrell & The Point, LLC

Golden Lasso, LLC

Lannan Foundation

Rhoady and Jeanne Marie Lee

National Endowment for the Arts

Cynthia Lovelace Sears and Frank Buxton

William and Ruth True

Washington State Arts Commission

Charles and Barbara Wright

To learn more about underwriting Copper Canyon Press titles, please call 360-385-4925 x103

The poems are set in Janson, revived by Herman Zapf in 1937 from the
original old-style serif typeface named for Dutch punchcutter and printer
Anton Janson. The headings are set in Franklin Gothic Extra Condensed.
Book design and composition by Phil Kovacevich. Printed on archival-
quality paper at McNaughton & Gunn, Inc.

The Chinese character for poetry is made up of two parts: "word"
and "temple." It also serves as pressmark for Copper Canyon Press.

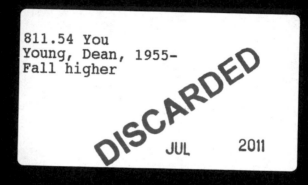